Inside Me an Island

Inside Me an Island

Poems
Lehua M. Taitano

WordTech Editions

Published by WordTech Editions
P.O. Box 541106
Cincinnati, OH 45254-1106

ISBN: 978-1-62549-283-8

Poetry Editor: Kevin Walzer
Business Editor: Lori Jareo

Visit us on the web at www.wordtechweb.com

ACKNOWLEDGEMENTS

Thank you to the editors of the following publications, in which many of these poems first appeared: *Fence, Lit Hub, The Offending Adam, Oxalis, Platte Valley Review, Poetry Magazine, Red Ink, Storyboard, Kinalamten Gi Pasifiku (Insights from Oceania)* and *Witness*. "Sonoma" was published as a chapbook by the generous editors of Dropleaf Press, to whom I owe special gratitude for their literary vision and kindness in the aftermath of the wildfires in Sonoma County.

Saina Ma'åse to fellow poets who have inspired, nourished, and otherwise encouraged me in the development of this work: Arlene Biala, July Hazard, Javier O. Juerta, Kaylee Dee Mendiola, Urayoán Noel, Carrie Ojanen, Barbara Jane Reyes, Craig Santos Perez, Tagi Qolouvaki, Aimee Suzara, and Angela Torres.

My utmost admiration goes to my mother, Catherine, and her siblings Josephine, Richard, and Rose Mary. Hu guiya hao! Rest in peace Joseph John and Susan Rose.

Cover artwork by Lisa Jarrett, from *Mother Tongues: 100 Exercises in Empathy, Part 3*. Courtesy of the artist.

Cover photograph of Maria Flores Taitano (Februrary 10, 1928 - January 4, 2000) on her 46th birthday, 1969. Taken by Josephine Taitano Sablan. Courtesy of Lehua M. Taitano.

This book is dedicated to my siblings, whose unconditional love and support sustain me. Leilani, David, Leah, Lydia, and Laura—you and the sea are my first memory.

Inside

Correspondence

Letter From an Island

(Maria Flores to Shelton Family, 1982.)

Hi everyone

I hope you are all fine

as for us we are

just fine

you ought to know how

I fill of writing

I'm not that good so please

excuse me I just make

this cookies for my girl

to remember the old lady

I think the baby cant

try it I have a gift and

her m__ one m_____

and I've other for Leah

and the shoes for Lehua

and the blouse I've buy

lady the mama is just

are 500 the blouse is 6 or

I hope you all like it

please write to me if you

recived it did you recived

the one that Lanie mail it

I ask Lanie and she said

she just mail it the other

day I want to thank you

for the meat

it really good

M___ give me a ring

but it fit on my small

finger please

don't tell her

that I'm giving you something

tell M___ if she want me

to come I'm ready

just

send my ticket

A Love Letter to the Chamoru People in the Twenty-first Century

Dear,

I will begin this in the middle, since all of my letters have always been to you, even if you haven't realized it. Go back and look. You'll see. All of my imaginings, my histories, my deaths and rebirths, my love and heartbreak. All of my words. My windblown hair, my lemon-sticky wrists. My fishbones, slings, feathers and offerings. My twig fires and heaped mounds of husks. My paint-dipped elbows and muddy feet. The bowers I weave into a home-scented bowl that might call you to me. The way I can sometimes chant down the sea and coax a wave to carry my heart to you. The salt on my thighs, the clutch of shells I carry in my deepest pockets. They are always for you. Addressed to you. So you'll understand, I hope, if I pick up where we last left off, which is always at horizon.

Who but a horizon so keenly feels how we are kept at each other's distance?

Because much more than wind carries so many of us away from our islands. Because we are made to consider our oceans as walls. Because we fumble the jar lid of tongues we've been made to bury. Because our sails have been burned. Because our grandmothers have been raped and worse. Because the bones of our beloved are being paved over and over with layers of poison and dollars that bear faces not our own.

Because the news tells us who we are not. Because our families are separated. Because distance means we cannot always conjure the scent of our auntie's cheek. Because we are visited by our ancestors in dreams. Because we are visited by our ancestors in waking life. Because our nieces and nephews struggle to remember the last time we visited.

Because two more of our sons and daughters have enlisted. Because their enlistment might return them home whole or in pieces or not at all. Because diabetes has taken another pair of our eyes. Because we cannot tread on pieces of our own land without clearance. Because we keep words like *clearance* and *deployment* and *strategic* and *stationed* in the bowl with our keys by the front door. Because we can count to a thousand in Spanish. Because we can count to the apocalypse in English.

Because our crow song has vanished. Because our trees are blighted. Because our reefs are targets. Because we are always in the path of military maneuvers. Because I must write this to you in English.

Because we are trending. Because our faces are lit up with the glow of emojis each shedding a single tear . Because our petitions do not go viral. Because Cara only half jokes about investing in bunker supplies. Because Michael is being fitted with a lapel mic for the twentieth time today. Because Clarissa splits herself open to talk story about Litekyan. Because Desiree is trying to ignore the planes flying overhead. Because Dåkot-ta is not even going to talk about anything but peace. Because Ned wants us to share with the world. Because Arielle is still trying to sell her atulai. Because Craig debates the value of visibility. Because our non-Chamoru friends text us to say what a shame but can they also get that kelaguin recipe?

Because we are shouting into the Pacific. Because our voices are choked in the fumes of B-1 bombers.

*

Because I could not sleep.

Because I could not eat.

Because I do not want to get my mind off things, I am writing to you.

I close my eyes against the morning sun in my garden—where I reach out to you across space and time—and I hear you. I hear you laughing and loving and crying. In despair and resistance. In anguish and abhorrence. What's more, I feel you. The salt in our blood carries droplets of the ocean. No matter where we are, inside us is a liquid web connecting our beating hearts.

I am quiet so I can perceive your tugs, the delicate density of your tangles.

And I want you to know that I am always scared, but I am always hopeful. Because I can feel you, I can feel our collective fear. We are proud, so we sometimes deny fear, keep it hidden like a lozenge under the tongue. We are resilient, so we know that it will dissolve. And when it does, we will still be here, tending our plants, casting our nets, shaping our canoes, writing our bodies into existence.

I am writing to you, mañe'lu, aunties, uncles, nenis, cousins, kin and all our saina.

I am writing to tell you that I see you. I hear you. I feel you. I love you. You matter.

I hope this letter finds you.

Until we can gaze together upon a horizon full of sails,
Lehua

Ma'te (Low Tide)

Shore Song

Our people

were shaped from stone

and

the pulsing

sea.

Sister's crouched

body

wave kneaded

salt   lapped

until   we tumbled

from her

of her   (of them)

                                                    all strong strong

            and

                              whole

together.   Birds

            regarded

                                        our sea foam

anklets

                                    our slippery ropes

        of hair our

cheeks   full
                          of

                                                    pebbles

        and scattered from the shore

        singing.

We opened

                                                                    our new

mouths

to

                        our

                                own   chorus

crooning

                                        SisterBrother

            we are

sun

                                                        moon

                sky

water

earth

all

siblings.

Create a sibling, a counterpart to your shale-flaked centerself, a blood-bound projection to visit you upon the lonely scree.

My brother says he is not a writer.

This means he writes for no one
but himself then burns the pages
with a kitchen match.

Sometimes, he writes for me.

This is a lie.
Onetime, he wrote for me.

The last blizzard he stretched to me,
astride two wheels laden with burro bundles—
blankets and jerky.

There's wind in South Dakota, he said. Lots of it.

Then he said, Badlands. They should name it

Davidlands now.

When he limped to my doorstep,
Montana November was glassed in
like sleep.

He uncurled
a lined notebook, belly warm.

I read with stomach sight.

>   *press closed clicking sap*
> *on a pine limb*
> >   *felt my head on a pole*
> > >   *with the moon in the river*
> *stareless eyes starless*
> > >   *eyes cast like die*

My heart tapped the glass. Our cadence, I said.
Yours and mine.

He fashioned his arms just so and said,
If you'll remember,

I used to cradle you for sixty spins
around the clockface.

A single minute less,
and you'd whimper awake.

A Walnut Tree

In the yard the green husks are sign enough. Deeper, an ink fouled black and maybe a white worm. Never walnuts. The kind mounded in wooden bowls. The silver claw bought special atop the scalloped white plate beside. Other families' tables. Where the chairs are cushioned and enough. Not so yours, where the fork scrape means you know nothing of respect. This is why you will never learn to be good.

A Night Crowded With Night

Box of blood or fist in a throat, when did you begin the swell? When we tiptoed in damp socks across the wood floor, the dust clung in increments of padding. There were times when I would beg a noise, the wrong pitch, the one that could seep a blister. The one that could puncture—deflation the craving fulfilled, the noiselessness of the after. White-socked feet in the dew night, creeping in the worm garden, my dim yellow light raised high.

They can sense your vibrations, worms. Will slip back into their loam tunnels, careening in their own slick skins before your thumb can think *pinch*.

A night crowded with night. A ghostly expansion of sound blooming beneath the eaves. Not the trees. Nor the wind. Nor any fluttering, hovering thing. No cat cry, no visceral ease. Sound without vessel or bloodbeat or breath.

I am saying I have heard the pitch of spectral aching rife with an immeasurable absence of marrow, the pulse and echo gone so long that time has plowed its memory into earth.

Come the Rain

when she was more whole she buried

    a book some kind of sin she knew

        a book plump with numbers

her heart the same and temptation easy

    as a tiptoe

        to lie and then bury the lie shallow

a few handfuls of dirt between

    greasy pages hands on a shovel and god

        hovering like a leaf shadow

a sidewalk a stone a bearing stuck

    and skin between

        what dismal luck to be tethered

or worse to think tethered when the chain's end's detached

    better to drag a swath behind she thinks but

        her voice boomed too loud in a space dumb

a roar in a jar a roar in a jar a roar

so back to the dirt

    like always it was red to bursting

and a silt in the binding then come the rain the dew
when all was excavated she

    said I will wear this like a stamp beneath my eyelids

      or deeper behind my tongue

I will carry what there is to be carried of shame

    because I haven't yet learned that

      shame should keep my

name out of its mouth.

Notes To A Sedentary Self

a time of creases
in, isolate island

blue akin
to the shelf where

once we met
raked shale, out

the ways of iron
glacier or knotted sheet

to preside over teeth, bones
a wherewithal

Islanders Waiting For Snow

The snow has not come

though our every deflation is

a chant for erasure.

Wind in our lungs we

huff, shiver its own drama,

the breath decibel one-tenth

a yelp. Concurrent, squint.

A cloud roils wing-black,

feinting puncture,

abdominal and swift.

White blanket, make

a desert of our nostalgia.

Unshouting, our desire

aches like a wedge.

One Way to Predict the Future

Heap fast a scrabble of doubts and call
it preparation, or better, stuff letters in a drawer
and blame silverfish for what's gone missing.

A collector's hinged maw still spares
voracity, as you are the pocks of your own extrapolation.

Through the wall stamp horse chestnuts
burr the ground while paper grass thick with rabbits
dusts a sketching,
a lusciousness like crafted graphite smudge.

There is a time of night when all of our sounds become animal.

When the threshold of sorrows shaves even
with woodcurl pleasure and the simplest
of push-button dreams coaxes the throat
to woof.

Spectator

oh, this soldier this soldier this

                                          he was shot down   could use

his body for oil

(because I am brown)   does she work have kids

        but all is subject to money

                       let me tell you about the firing ranges

(oh, you are from *insert assumption)

your passport next time but today, since you have cash

                                                    We

the party

(Coco Fusco, you've heard?)

        it's a celebration when all the flags are flying

                                      (like Pyramus and

Thisbe?)

I got a casserole to take over later

his wife is pregnant, bless her heart

food not bombs food not
bombs food

(I heard you're searching for a heart of glass)

(is it Ocean-a or Ocean-i-a)

such shame when them's that
don't got hafta go off

(beautiful, your skin can I slip this off you) in a real cage, and the
children were the most sincere ones

[[[[[spectaculum]]]]]

nah dude like an urban homesteader, where the rain catchments corner
the house it's legit

after all speak

Laws his mama's over there

this shit makes me so effity effing sick

                    (no, seriously in a cage)   fight not out of fear but
we're held up here in the road, honey it's like a parade with flags

            look the
helicopters

                                        from age eight to age damn

(hula hula hulahoop is one I've heard)
                        I lived there, once
                                    my daddy has southern roots

it's all just a little bit a ball and chain

                                        (Acercate a mi)

(yours is the softest i've felt)
                    four, six, and ten I think
                        plus the baby
                                            I think
Afghanistan
a spring sky to beat all

39

(because I am brown because you are brown)

all the family's supporters are here and the hearse

                                                    patriotism
is the new

(they spoke gibberish and the people fed them bananas)

(Coco)
        do you need help with that step back now

a six-month-old   his legs were blown clean
off like

        blam
            Dolly Parton is like Gaga's grandmother

(he said 'you ever live in a hut')

(people are so disgusting)

(you really are spectacular)

problematic Egypt and it started like this, with food

                                        (Acercate?)

        I ain't slept and I need a bed

                                                        yes
sir, because we don't
support fascists

        (I've never been with a woman like this)

walls are there for a reason

                                    shush up they're about to

sing

the star spangled

Speak *father, father, father, father, father, father* until the
story surfaces of your unravel.

algebra always between us

I did it right once correct—correctly

in the factor field all thistle
I spied the single clover pressed it between my knees

my imitations mingling mangled
his four (triangled tulip canted, planted)
his nine (six's shadow reversed in a pool placid)

his carpenter's pencil never scrawled
—eraserless—

I swayed and plied while he calculated
invisibility

slantways the bucknife thumbjamb peeled the driest scent
(yellow-edged woodcurl)

sheaves fluttered to graph paper a heap soon
scooped a tinder pile huddle

mercurochrome stains a scab the way
sunspots maim
a mole

his mottled palm on my shoulder
the thumbnail a hammered
plum

conferred little but
heat

Your Distraction was Mechanism

Slow love. The kind who slips beneath the river rock (oval, your heart) on
a day pressed with drizzle and gnat cloud. You were busying yourself
with tracks, thumbing clay—crayfish leavings, a burrow excavated in
spheres. Leg-worked. Meanwhile, your distraction was mechanism, your
eyes lost conjuring jointed legs ushering a path. Precision their wake.
While you were counting revolutions. Love eased like liquid, slackened so.
Hummed for your heart's dry socket. At the edge of your ellipse.
Searching the grain spaces.

Have mercy on a creature who does not yet know your face.

Behind double panes
on the fifth floor

the university's corner of poetry cabinets
curled COUGAR in a jar before I broke
the lock.

Unclassified, it
in simplest preservation is fetal
potentiality

hovering like a comma,
spine furred.

Of course one thinks the pine perch,

purr the sound
of stones tumbling.

One thinks fang sink.

(∩)

The library has shelved it:

Chordata Mammalia Carnivora Felidae

A period piece, a baubling curiosity—
(also PUMA, MOUNTAIN LION)

(∩)

We had thoughts, Puma concolor and I:

I have visions of your rest.
Yes.

Beneath ridge tree cupped in grass.
Yes.

We'll splinter the jar, bathe you in creek water—

Yes—

Wrap you in lightest muslin
Yes, and sage—

Yes, white sage, yes. And orange star buds and leaves and—
Yes.

And these words, too, in my griefscrawl?

Stone tumble.
Stone tumble.
Stone tumble.
Stone tumble.

Banana Queen

The middle of Everywhere is what I said
to this one who asked Where.

Instead of Nowhere, which he claimed.

Find it he said, on this map here.
Do.

All the cartography in his world could
not make it anything more than a gnat hole.

Injun, this other one said. Must be, with a name like that.

(All they are ever trying to get at is what
flavor should we call your cunt.)

You don't look like—this other one
said
—a Guamanite.
(Guamish. Guamese. Guamarian.) Foster, another one said.
Bananas.

He couldn't palate

my aversion, which is truest allergy, cramped.

With a name like that,

he said, I'd think you'd be The Banana Queen.

(   )

Should I pluck each injury like an arrow and dis- mantle each and if so
how.

Besides which wounds deepest, the point

or the nock.

Anyway my quivers are deep as hulls and

the ocean rocks the clatter magicking feather to

fish bone.

Then waves shudder and each

vertebra is a vowel each

rib an inflection

until each white shard

knits itself into a slight poem,

into a swimming skeleton of everything

I could ever say

at all.

Trespass

this morning the neighbor with the silken car
must've slid his cents

into mine said please do
not park in front of my house

or property and *not* of course <u>CAPITALIZED</u>
<u>UNDERLINED</u> on a business card

guess he works at this
bank does something calculative while the

scrawny guy across the sidewalk showed
up post marathon

training with sweat rope legs and
saw it go down—

me taking the soggy expletive
from the wiper

blade though he didn't let
on he saw but it was a
puncture somehow some deflation
of the day before it really

began to know this brick and
vinyl town of cul de sacs do you know it means
bottom of the bag

is another replica some outfit of the same
white squatters with stiff wide elbows keeping
the lines and lines in this gridded way saying

know your place brown I've worked for this grass
stamp my whole life
(or not) and the fuck
 if your little shit self is gonna encroach
yes yes that's the word *encroach*

with your hooks and and and your tight jeans
your dented truck

your late night ways

Retrace the landscape, where you have sieved earth for stones or scent alone.

for Katie Kane

We stalk the patch of grass. Swish and swingle. Tunnels curl between bunches below the breathless hill. We avoid participle, no –ing because it passive-fies, makes a quality of have, not the have itself. I don't ask permission, though at day's end it is not as simple as mine not

mine. I eye the exposure in berms that speaks bobsled, skeleton. A creature shapes its way. You stab at the vole's futility, say look at its conspicuousness, its foolish filet of earth, its obvious scramble! It digs with its hands, shares kinship blindness. Trust me. It feels the hem of wind on its back, the light shaft prick. It senses hawk claw, coyote stamp. It perseveres in its must.

Before you spoke vole, I dubbed the hills behind the house Mouse Trap. Simple drab ignorance. (All scampering is not the same.) What trappings droppings graying can. What censures down mounds to the epicenter shrine, what humming magic transforms fur to fur, scamper to tunnel and dig dig dig. We climb, glean, retrieve some loss across ridge rife, across bone bleach. Look! the double car garage edges the grass. The sink and dip, the rise. I claim it. Mine. As does the dog. She pisses on barbed wire, effulgent gush on twist caught with hair, earth, the ruff of your shirt. We claim all we see, don't see the dog is dying. Liver the size of a punch. After the sun, in the kitchen— pronunciation, movement, women's solace. A firm bamboo roll gathering density's bundle. We dip our fingers in the water bowl for absolution before we press the rice. If I had a cloak I would bundle grasses. Let the unfed be continually fed. I want comfort, a deer mattress, a heart stuffed with trample.

And All of Them for Love (Four Wishes)

A crevice and from it, lava. Seabirds swore they eyed a flume of seed, but the ocean quivered and all was wash.

Ashore, someone thought they caught a glimpse of the baby before she slipped beneath a final, quiet wave. Saw her crown licked with salt, a swirl of her black hair thick with seven o'clock sun.

That day, the tide was neap. (The steady tugging imperceptible.)

Baby girl swaddled in kelp, newest eyes scouring the well of sky—one fixed upon the thumbnail moon, the other lost in the curdle of sun.

A span of four breaths and the fourth one saturate. Little tip of tongue searching the throat for sound.

I thought there would be something, she bubbled. Something to float me.

Belly full of sea suckle. Lungs, too. She swooned into the depths, closed her eyes and heard the tinny music rising.

The Seat of Heaven

the task of withholding is not so much

an exercise in patience as re-imagining space

they want to love her but a rope is a line

is a folded box full of circles

to tongue-tip asceticism is not the same

as knowing a tincture a rope

is a river she has no appetite

for iron

a river is folded

a chest of sun left unlatched

finds its way to the delta

Hafnot (High Tide)

Low Mountain Lake Song

Summer's hem. The moon, a swelling. Too, bullfrog throats, vibrating across the slick green bay. Full low like a plump lip jug pressing. At night, this side of things is settled without the memory of ache. Even the shallows are pregnant. Slow fish, the terrapin's slide. In the trees, a ladder to nowhere. A fire for the color of it, the air warmer than smoke. A cupping, an ease, a drifting you want to pocket.

Past midnight, the crescent of green water holds, tongue warm. The boat green, the shore grass green. Flute green the swamp reeds. Green the unseen frogs, the firefly pulse. Beneath the mouth of a moonbright sky, sway. Spilt green, the moment before a song. A song, green, silt green in the lungs.

One Kind of Hunger

The Seneca carry stories in satchels.

They are made of pounded corn and a grandmother's throat.

The right boy will approach the dampness of a forest with a sling, a modest twining wreath for the bodies of birds. A liquid eye.

When ruffed from leaves, the breath of flight is dissolute.

What else, the moment of weightlessness before a great plunge?

In a lost place, a stone will find the boy.

Give me your birds, she will say, and I will tell you a story.

A stone, too, admits hunger.

The boy is willing. Loses all his beaks.

What necklace will his grandmother make now.

The sun has given the stone a mouth. With it, she sings of what has been lost.

She sings and sings and sings.

An Oiled Groove

Here is an unfinished story of grief exposed.
Joy, after the brink.

Some basic elements:
contempt
an immutable bond
the sort of disruption worth mentioning
irreversible action

A secret comes to surface.
(Evitable.)

Visualize a likely context.
Let's say there's a current, closed.

This electric circular route. And joy racing
its oiled groove.

Previous, the wires

hammered, twisted, married.

Copper can house a memory
if someone's hands are involved.

A groove must wear thin or else dusts with disuse.
Either way, a disintegration.

Because the thing cannot hold the thing itself.
(Joy.)

Because hands are not enough.
We break down.

Some Don't Have To Ask

for July

When I first saw him, he had already planned his escape. Turquoise boots and a dandy mustache. Goodwill vest, summer slacks. I swaggered in, river slick and cool to make a point, with L twining my left arm. Palms all filament. What a pair, we. How everyone was wing drawn.

Anyway, he was slipping through the cracks—a concerted effort—and L and I, well. We spotted him right away, wrote three acts in glances. Loose tobacco on our lips. Pidgin for yes. A conflagration of assumptions. He hatched his name with a feathered tongue. What could we do but swoon.

Bare your back to outside air. To sun if it's a Sunday.
Recline with a friend or stand-in. Trust with your skin.
Loose ten lines for transcription. Across your spine,
scapulae, your dorsal rib pinch, tender.

unseasonable februrary goldmine sky and the hens
in their coop number three or four

a blue heeler and housemates pick
over chicken bones bleached in

the white soup pot
crackle dry is the compost mound

we use a chair backwards and ladder easel
for the beercan cigarette

i peel two february shirts, a black bra
shiver and straddle

the chair while he smokes behind
with one hand, the other

poised with stolen revlon eyeliner
lining capitals

we get to sunshine
and he asks line break?
yes

one stanza and the house women hoot, say
i love when my yard is full of naked women

though i am only one

the eyelid pencil is so soft, thin i think
maybe for a moment we are rehearsing

then they all gather semicircle—
the women the heeler the hens—

and read in unison

inside and later on a hip-high table
a photograph of four chickens

my scribe, he points
to one and three and says

dead and dead

Enchanted Rock, Texas

Time we reach the flower fields, the battery's spent.
Capture, my basic need.

A slick rock cliffs to cactus scrub
and bottom gnarl.

What I would frame is projection.

Hawk wings pressing a shadow flat across currents.
(How sea-like the sky.)

I have a jointed leg and tremble
the ascension in clutches.

Scrape and jam up into a long split of stone, summon
pillow, compression and somehow
the guts of a slim, cool fish.

Then tumble presses in, slip hot
on her heels.

The wind is only a scent circle.
Mesquite or shock of salt kelp.

When the birds are gone, a plank bridge,
a dry wash pier.

Desert quiet me
in the night, crossing
with skirt steps, the lantern swinging.

What Mountain Birds Will Keep

flung was a net

supple grid
across bare tracts
            so

snagged my thighs on every
            glistening
corner turned to find

each plot a tin
            set
to rust then

the rains cleaved
clouds split by
an old magic
            I
can see only

with a mind bent

on branches drought
      seed
bone clack

circles birthed from
      circles

Kituwah

For Ching Fu

reservation river,
and the incremental
trestles criss
cross the broken flag tree
signaling the creek where
villas sell for half
the asking.

remember when
I posed with the stuffed
black bear
outside the fudge shop?
at six, I came away
with that polaroid, a toy
tom-tom and a blooming
disquietude.

we weren't yet

friends.

that was when
the pond was swollen
with prize fish,
when half-baited hooks
would snag any flap
of fin or gill,
and the boy at the wooden
counter hefted
a lead pipe with his striking hand.

I think the sign read:
Whole in the Morning,
Filleted by Nightfall.

but now we slip
on the cobbled bank pitched
toward the olive lip of
bridge water
and the cars are all mangled,
wedged carefully across
the stream.

silvered bumpers
piled in the pattern
of surrender,
the roadside having shrugged
them over the rails.

how neat the battering,
how organized the rusted
lament.

not far from this place,
just downstream,
we will stumble upon
Kituwah,
move quietly through her
barren cornfields,
sing silently
our prayers.

A Curse Dismantled Via a Facile Understanding of Photonics

Seven stop signs, and each with a bullet-sieved pattern.

Right place, right time if you're the one
who gets to watch.

A celestial backlight might align three, say,
and the punctured illumination on the shadowed
curb will resemble a woman's face.

In such situations everyone will dispute the coincidence though no one
can deny her chin is uncannily
shaped like a papaya.

One day the tilt of things will make sense.

\\\

A good time to try out your absurd postulations is beneath blankets with a warm lover.

For one, the mouth is cozier.

Begin with
some finer poet's architectural
verse then let slip

I don't believe in constellations

Draw up a pillow
and breathe into it your

stale water breath
cyclone the sheets hum

There can never be silence absolute

When those radiant hands skim the breadth
of your outstretched torso gasp

The more I am bruised, the less capacity I have for love

Smoking in the Window of My New Lover's Kitchen

seafoam kitchen cabinets the ledge
before the roofs' layered grip

pitch aslant and bamboo wind
blades the urchin fan yields
an effortless spinning

a nest bent careening
with warmth smooths worry to
concavity a bowl a bell a
depth eased upward

song tousled about the lungs until
linoleum squares are glossed
to beige the knives all left-
facing

brushed table saucer squat
tablet reminders in paper
sheets thin as news
ink eager with blue

icebox rank with melt yet
the dog's nose more
defunct his white white ears flick

silent wing beats a moth a
bat's filmy way he is
never settled

heavy cream gone to clump
butter today the cast iron empty
but tomorrow
perhaps

Come Sit Around This Stone

The International Hotel, Manilatown, San Francisco, April 21, 2016

for Aimee, Angela, Arlene, Barbara Jane, Javier, and Urayoán

Kuwentuhan! Kuwentuhan!

                                        What stories on the corner

of Jackson

                        which exhumes   Tubman, strata,

press   of time

                                        beneath sidewalks stained

today

with piss,   yesterday's blood.
Batons

polished,   bullets,
helmets,   the same

            backdrop,

                        the burst

on loop on loop on loop:

I only want

to see you

Across,   the House of Nanking,   a man
in   khaki   head-to- toe

scooping paper   and

        soggy   pigeon
        mess.

East/West Bank.

    I only want to see you   on loop on
loop on loop:

 49 mile   scenic   drive

            LED man   housed in   a
box, mid-stride

crossing,

    See you standing
super imposed   orange
         ticking

    countdown   to   Kearny.

             Exhume
this brickscape,

the signs are   flashing   move
move move.

                                         I only want

to see you

Police   crusade   on
horseback,   beating stick a

        casual   caress   and
      the horse's

                        eye, stuttering.

            See you laughing

Leaflets   newsprint   scrawl spitting   rain
     khaki man   bends to
       a   parcel   and we

were talking of Tubman.
                   Will her face   imprint
       on any policy
more   than   a

sheaf.

On loop on loop:
purple

              the corner of Jackson   *10,000*
carabaos,   a   newer version

                                          laughing

            of the same old dark

the brick canvas
exhumed,   a rifle

thrusts   up   through   asphalt   pooled
               with   rain-diluted
              urine.

    God
damnit.

God   damnit.

purple, purple, purple, purple, purple, purple, purple

At   eight-   forty   -eight
International,

                   a corner enfolding
tableau:

this bed frame   of brown
poetas,   the thrum of
  the

                   unearthed   (here Harriet's rifle juts

up from beneath the sheets).

Here,   the Bay Shore Fish
Wharf,   Great Saigon

                   move
move   move

I only want to see you

quickly,   Kobe Bento,
                                  move!

          laughing in the

                    Nightstick   slick with

rain.

Here On The Seam

Here on the seam it is easy to
stitch a poem from debris—
biting fly and fence post fags up
from the city december slant
sun glittering the wedged tire, the
radioactive shore.

How delicious the salt suture, the lapping ache.

It Is The Other Time

I wake up and another poet has died
and wonder how many people are affected
Really am I

≤

Back home I visited the baby who recognized me some
She put my necklace in her mouth then mine

I gave the baby a book about excess
as illustrated by a superb magpie

≤

The woman's face was strange in the absurd light of my helmet
I concerned myself with the glare

She was already crying
the woman

≤

The baby does gymnastics now and can ride a scooter
down a slide

The dog gets out of the way
quick

≤

The people who care about the poet probably
don't know his middle name
I'm not saying I do

≤

A nightly succession of dreams cataclysmic:

Waves transmogrified the back of a runaway
truck speeding rearward toward a tree
funnel clouds the crumble of solid ground

We're going to die out here I said to my faceless
companions

≤

The store where I work is having another sale
Get dialed in says my boss Get dialed in

≤

I don't usually take that road home but minor
adjustments led me to an intersection

She didn't even see me she
blurbled

≤

Baby
the baby can say along with about
any other thing

≤

I speak to almost no one about poetry capital P I
have edged out of that circle I
get dialed in

$\leq$

She had to have seen me
The intersection was lit

There are seconds and there are
half seconds

The lady wore a pink fleece
It's all my fault she sobbed Do
you want to come sit in my car

$\leq$

The baby has ten teeth maybe
if I had to guess

One got popped out caught
in the tab of a Coca Cola can
but the doctor put it back in

The magpie has an ankle tag thanks
to an artist with intention

≤

The news tells me the poet lived close by I
guess I should have known

≤

I paddled a huge board
though I don't know really
how

to surf I am conversing
with my eclipsing fears

≤

It's the capital that keeps the circle close
a half second is all
it takes

The woman wanted me to console her for the Almost
I could have killed you she blurbed

The magpie carries a marble
wrapped in ribbon

The baby will surely
like that later

The storm kept the locals away

Current ignorant I got sucked out to sea
My heart bobbingly

Get dialed in Champ says my boss
in earnest for the big sale

I had a rhythm going pedaling
in the night

The intersection was lit well
my heart an octopus in flight

The woman hugged me, her perfume
and fleece one stuffy synthetic

I almost I almost I

Beneath me the board and swell
a monstrous movement I had not known

Rain salt spray and the wind
erasing

The baby says sit to the dog
and me alike

Bird on a Limb Poem

this morning ocean clouds
an apologetic rain
and the chickens next
door haggle over mustard seeds corn
the driest eucalyptus
limb

I would like to parcel up one
blackbird's plummet skim
with one fingertip that perfectly ragged
wound that red red throat
upon a slender dark
wing

Estuary

Something like love found me. I did not tell anyone. Or I did, but the words turned to birdsong on my tongue. (Her name? When the body cannot contain the heart.) An estuary carries letters. Lovely script, trailing, sinuous. Backlit in blue pulse.

The feathered word that hums about us, between us, is *unmoored*. What we share. Roots of the air. (My name? The flower.) Half this, half that. The great sea has set me in motion, set me adrift, moving me like a weed in the brine river. I have the letters.

(Our names? Both exchanged, for the sake of our grandmothers. We could not take up their tongues because their song is part of what we lost.)

Weeping bloom. With/out. Here's what the letters contain: boats, oceans, currents, moons, flowers, nests. Unnamed shades of love. We are soil-less, too. (Tai tano.) She reached across the map, set a bloom adrift in the surf to wish my healing. In the bed for weeks, my snapped knee a misshapen breadfruit, I lolled in a lightless chasm. All the while willing a string of petals to unfurl from my chest—the longest lei seeking her across oceans. Did it find her. She says my name is everywhere she looks. Little red flowers, rarer yellow. Both/and. Blossoms, street signs. The stars, the ocean, the green, green trees, winged things, flowers, earth, sky, rain. Her name is everywhere I close my eyes. The upward welling, when the heart persists.

How can you miss what you have never held? I have seen her pictures. Something about her eyes. My last love, her mouth. In dreams I construct a lover of parts. She sees, she sings. But one cannot chance the bird.

In dreams I have everything. In my palms. The bird, the pinfeather dust. The havenot breathing as one.

In dreams I am the flower me—all flush and nectar—the bees' humming in my cheeks.

Sonoma Prelude

Cultural resource studies in the Lake Sonoma Area began in 1964, when Adan Treganza, an archaeologist from San Francisco State College, and his small crew surveyed the area for prehistoric sites. Although several sites were found during their brief reconnaissance, none was judged important enough to warrant excavation. Construction began on the Warm Springs Dam in 1967. (Praetzellis, Praetzellis, and Stewart. *Before Warm Springs Dam: A History of the Lake Sonoma Area*, 1985)

I stuffed a sack with two days' worth of warmth, food and light and slid a slender boat onto the waters of Lake Sonoma almost immediately upon arriving at my new home in Northern California. I was alone, familiar with no one or nothing, not yet comfortable with the word *Californian*. I had just driven three-thousand miles in a zagging path across springtime America. I was in love maybe, was still healing from physical and emotional trauma, maybe, and was definitely in dire need of myself.

For me, always, there is some quality of being adrift that serves to center. To be afloat is to be at once in and out of control, a condition in which one can drop a plumb line of consciousness into uncertain depths and test the tautness of adaptability, the sway of emotional well being. To be from an island yet to exist off-island is to continually reconcile the waters.

So I found a boat. And a lake. And I thought of the way the lake had come to be. And the way of history that floods and flushes out those who would call the land at the bottom of the lake home. And the stories and languages of those displaced people—the Pomo, the Miwok—whose sacred sites were drowned to make the place where boats like mine could float above on any given Wednesday in spring. Which made me think of my own displacement and of being in maybe love too, which is to say— of living still and seeking happiness still, and of finding a new home in a land not my own in the middle of the ache of being one who is displaced and alone with myself.

On the banks of that flooded place, I wrote the love letter *Sonoma*. The elegy *Sonoma*. The maybe long poem *Sonoma*. The floating words swirling in a canoe *Sonoma*, for my brothers and sisters adrift.

Sonoma

I will say golden and I will say turn. light,
I'll utter, and also gulf.

                                    stubble, you should know. and
shake

too, the upward flick of sound you might swallow.

water shadow. lichen.
the nose of a swimming creature,
slick.

                    a nest on the slenderest creak. shirk. a slant dance.

there is a filling.

...

folding soft itch. hollow tap.

I will say madrone. I will say breath in
a bowl crowned with leaves.

                                        you will want to know clack

and possibly slump, but who can say. like as not, you'll swoon
bay crazy for olive.

                        olive.

who wouldn't want a word like that.

...

I could mutter gosling.

        chelated, it's true. mirage. so.

I will let you in on joist and sheet.

        (when is there not a surface.)

better, I will say chord. aviary.

slow hoof and this: plush.

I have ears in my throat.

loft.

...

you are humming, tell true.

I have ears.

I have ears in my throat. which is to say

I will say slender unctuous sway and then pebbled

clay

viscous dram.

you will guess whiskey

and steel cup.

you will guess the time
of day.

...

                                        you might ask

chute.

I will say needle. I will say pull
            pull pull and

                              slake wash sift.

you will ask for simple.

simple.

...

I will tell you a story.

People wish to contain a river. To slide in a wall as if the banks were grooved and push back a flowing river. As if to staunch a wound.

You are a tree on the bank and suddenly, the flood. Now your branches are bare, riddled with tapping. Now you are bleached and ghostly. Submerged shipwreck, your tongue-soft roots.

...

you will ask for more.

I will say nutria or muskrat.

                                                                    the

slick nose.

I can divulge candle.

                        you will seem to me a feather.

            I will croon.

            I have ears in my throat.

simple.

...

push   flume glass   plump quell   thorax
    swish   wilt   crisp   antennae
mince   belt   dilate   hone
    harmonium   aplomb   click
        scuttle

...

skip.

...

I will tell you a story.

The night we met we did not want each other. This is what we said with our hands. They cupped and shuffled. They rolled and tapped. Not we, they said. Not now, no.

So we waited for the ice to shift. Glacial, we.

...

you will ask for more.

                                                    more.

              moths, more. months, more. shadow of hand on pages,

more.

you might blink.

                       levered wings, more.

chitter chitter lantern, yes.

       more.

...

I can now say pig.

it deserves more.

pig!

but I can give you kettle. wool cheek, the right weight.
I can say gristle and hatch.

filament, yes. it's true.

…

my dreams have ears.

you turn over eagle

hysteria and wind. oh, the wind.

      I will give you channel.

                                    you pirouette in a satin
bloom.

simple.

you sideways and slip.
bloom.

I will say root.

…

I will tell you a poem.

…

glade.

…

you will want to sing,
tell me.

I will hum blue blue blue and also

                                                                    oh
oh then bulb.

…

I am not caught. netlessly.

                                                you will ask cast.

yes. I will say yes.

            golden plumb cadence wrung salt
lush abatement.

...

I can tell you hours. disc.

      stone and caw and craw and squinch and scritch and reed and

...

           you, spinning bloom. I am more than settled silt.

I am aglide

(when is there not a surface.)

...

you will ask for eyes.

      I will give you

orbital.

orbital.

...

      currents slick a trillion
glints osprey breeze

two men trolling slow

                     offer me a beer I took

two.

...

I did not need a fire.

...

I will sigh pawprints.

scratch and toe and lever.

twist.

you, lovely bloom.

...

I will call their names.

                                        beetle. tick. damsel. magpie. turtle.
vulture.

I dreamt two turtles. one attacking the other.

tender necks.

…

simple.

one did not
make it.

gush.

…

you will ask for eyes.

I can give you script.

...

aslant. take two and

                                                call me.

...

flip.

...

are you ready for olive.

...

my dreams have ears.

hyena, I always spit. my dreams say wolf.

(neither.)

...

more.

sun more and gaze more. mocha. spoon, more. riffle.

                                                            you
are quiet and

seated.

I will be chaff or ivy.

...

the thing about being your own motor is

                    you're your own motor.

the men laugh trollingly.

...

a river can be contained.

I am always sided with delta.

...

no hummock withstood or rather was standing enough.

island-lessly.

...

you are sitting patiently.

                                        my dreams have breath.

a single curl nearest your nape rustles.

        simple.

    ...

you will know me by my sway.

    ...

you do not ask

so

                                       I can give without wedge.

the key is on the sill.

…

I will say drink ellipses buoy skim yawp

                                                wooshingly

recline.

you, quiet bloom

satin seated.

more.

…

                you sideways.

glacial flow exquisite.

the thing about being your own motor—

…

you don't have to ask.

swell.

NOTES

"Letter from an Island" (*The Offending Adam*) is a transcription of a handwritten letter sent by Maria Flores Taitano to the Shelton family in 1982. Elisions and omissions reflect the legibility and translational nuances of the text, interpreted by the author.

"A Love Letter to the Chamoru People in the "Twenty-first Century" (*Kinalamten Gi Pasifiku (Insights from Oceania)*) was also featured on the radio program "It's Lit with PhDJ," KTUH FM, Honolulu, hosted by Anjoli Roy. An archived recording of the author's reading can be found at: https://itslitwithphdj.wordpress.com

"Spectator" (*Fence*) consists of fragments taken from overheard conversations at a roadside funereal parade for a U.S. soldier in Mills River, North Carolina, on the afternoon of his remains being returned to his family; overheard conversations at an anti-war rally in downtown Asheville, North Carolina; and remembered fragments of an exchange between the author and an unrequited love interest.

"Create a sibling...", "Speak *father father father*...", "Have mercy on a creature...", "Retrace the landscape...", and "Bare your back..." (*Witness / Platte Valley* Review) are from a series of somatic poems in which the titles represent directions for somatic poetry exercises. They are designed to be accessible to any person, regardless of the nature or condition of their bodies.

"One Kind of Hunger" (*Poetry*) is the author's retelling of a story (the content of which explains the origin of stories) told to her in her youth by a teenage friend from the Seneca Nation. The story itself, coupled with a formative encounter of sharing oral cultural traditions with another indigenous friend in a predominantly white, Southern town, continues to nourish the author's work.

"Come Sit Around This Stone" was written at Kuwentuhan (Talkstory): A Project of the Poetry Center at SFSU and Barbara Jane Reyes, on the morning of the group's convening, which happened to coincide with Prince's death.

"Banana Queen" (*The Offending Adam*) was written in response to the author's encounter with a coworker and his use of racist language in a conversation about dessert.

"Here on the Seam" is a transcription of the author's earth poem, etched into sand at Steep Ravine Beach in Marin County, California.

ABOUT THE AUTHOR

Lehua M. Taitano is the author of *A Bell Made of Stones* (poems, TinFish Press) and the chapbooks *appalachiapacific*—winner of the Merriam-Frontier Award for short fiction—and *Sonoma* (Dropleaf Press).

Her literary and interdisciplinary art have been featured at APAture (Kearny Street Workshop), Kuwenthuhan: A Project of the Poetry Center at SFSU and Barabara Jane Reyes, and 'Ae Kai: A Culture Lab on Convergence (The Smithsonian Institute's Asian Pacific American Center). A queer, native Chamoru from Yigo, Guåhan (Guam), she lives in California, where she also works as a bicycle mechanic.

83561979R00083

Made in the USA
San Bernardino, CA
27 July 2018